James Lorimer & Company Ltd., Publishers acknowledges the support of the Ontario Arts Council. We acknowledge the financial support of the Government of Canada through the Canada Book Fund for our publishing activities. We acknowledge the support of the Canada Council for the Arts which last year invested $24.3 million in writing and publishing throughout Canada. We acknowledge the Government of Ontario through the Ontario Media Development Corporation's Ontario Book Initiative.

Cover design: Meredith Bangay
Cover image: Matt Boulton (top), Fanny Schertzer (bottom)

Library and Archives Canada Cataloguing in Publication

Irwin, Sue, 1963-, author
    Safety stars : players who fought to make the hard-hitting game of professional hockey safer / Sue Irwin.

Issued in print and electronic formats.
ISBN 978-1-4594-0847-0 (bound).--ISBN 978-1-4594-0846-3 (pbk.).--
ISBN 978-1-4594-0848-7 (epub)

    1. Hockey--Safety measures--Juvenile literature. 2. Hockey--
Equipment and supplies--Juvenile literature. 3. National Hockey
League--Juvenile literature. I. Title.

GV848.35.I78 2015   j796.962'640289   C2014-907509-X
C2014-907510-3

James Lorimer & Company Ltd., Publishers
317 Adelaide Street West, Suite 1002
Toronto, ON, Canada
M5V 1P9
www.lorimer.ca

Distributed in the United States by:
Orca Book Publishers
P.O. Box 468
Custer, WA USA
98240-0468

Printed and bound in Canada.
Manufactured by Marquis in Montmagny, Quebec in February 2015.
Job # 111637

To my brothers,
Les and Alex,
whose hockey tournaments
were a highlight of my
weekends as a teen, and to
Daniel, whose goalie rookie
card I'll always treasure

Contents

Prologue

This is it, Jacques thought. *Finally, the chance I've been waiting for.*

It was November 1, 1959. The New York Rangers were hosting the Montreal Canadiens, the most powerful team in the league. The sold-out crowd sat silent in Madison Square Garden. Everyone was thinking the same thing: *What's going to happen to Montreal's goalie?*

In the first aid room, goalie Jacques Plante lay still on the stretcher. It even hurt to blink, but he couldn't help it. The lights glared down. He winced. Blood spurted from the wound on his face, trickled onto his neck, and stained his white jersey.

Moments before, Jacques had given New York's Andy Bathgate a poke check. This move sent Andy headfirst into the boards. Angry and embarrassed, Andy was determined to get even. At his first chance, he shot the puck straight at the Montreal goalie's head. The puck just missed Jacques's left eye, but left a long gash running from the corner of his mouth, up, and through his nostril.

A sportswriter described what he saw next. "Plante promptly sprawled on his stomach, his head cushioned in an ugly pool of blood. Bathgate raced to the fallen goalie and lifted his head. Blood poured from the wound onto the New York player's fingers. It was obvious that this was serious stuff . . ."

Shocked, the 15,000 fans in the arena watched Jacques stand up with the help of his teammates, and skate off the ice. News reporters crowded around, getting as close as they dared. They watched as, according to one journalist, "the doctor scraped away bits of loose flesh from the wound before inserting the stitches. Plante lay there, soundless, his fingers locked, as the needle knifed through the raw flesh."

It was the first period of the game, and there was a lot of game time left. Coach Toe Blake needed his team to win tonight. He had led the Montreal Canadiens to win the Stanley Cup four times in a row. Even though it was early in the season, he couldn't stand the thought of losing a single game to New York — the team in second-last place.

Finally, he spoke. "Wear your mask for the rest of the game, if you like."

With his gums still bleeding, Jacques said, "I wouldn't go back without it."

"You know I don't like it," Blake snapped. "But I need you out there. And as soon as this cut heals, you won't be wearing that mask anymore. You can be sure of that!" Then he turned and stormed out of the room.

When the doctor finished his job, Jacques didn't waste any time. He carefully put on his mask and made his way back to the ice.

1 A Dangerous Game

Hockey, Canada's favourite sport, is fast and sometimes vicious. Players need to be on the lookout for all kinds of danger. Pucks whiz past them. Sticks swing high around them. Razor-sharp skate blades slice across the ice below them. All around them, opponents do anything it takes to win.

Since it was first played, the game has changed in many ways. Even team uniforms have changed. In the beginning, players were more concerned about warmth than safety. Back then, the sport was played on outdoor rinks. So players wore heavy wool sweaters to keep warm. Wet with sweat, the uniforms became even heavier.

Now, hockey gear is all about speed and protection. Today's fully dressed National Hockey League (NHL) player is covered in equipment that offers head-to-toe safety. You might think he looks like a Star Wars character — a well-dressed one, that is, in custom-fit, lightweight materials. Uniforms and gear don't weigh today's athletes down. They can move quickly and easily. Thin, "breathable" jerseys keep them cool and comfortable. Clean, dry clothing also protects them from infection.

At first, the only thing that players wore for safety was shin guards. This was all they had to shield them from pucks and sticks. In time, they began guarding their shoulders, elbows and knees, too.

In the early 1930s, Montreal's Babe Siebert broke his thumb. His trainer put a shoehorn in his glove to protect his thumb. A safer glove was invented because of this trainer's clever idea.

Felt and leather elbow pads made way to hard bare plastic or fibreglass. Shoulder pads were like the ones worn by football players. Soon, players began to be harmed by other players' equipment! In 1950, NHL president Clarence Campbell noticed. He announced to the media, "It is completely ridiculous for us to permit one player to protect himself with . . . equipment which is constructed in a manner which can injure another." Again, changes needed to be made.

Today, Coach Lindy Ruff thinks safety should be the number-one goal. He told a reporter, it's "the proper thing to do."

Viktor Stalberg, forward for the

Jock or Jill?

More girls are playing hockey now than ever before. Sadly, big business hasn't kept up. Some companies are just beginning to make hockey pants, pelvic protectors, and skates for girls. But all players need gear that fits their size and shape.

Chicago Blackhawks, remembers his first pair of hockey pants. They were too big, and they didn't come with suspenders. Laughing, Viktor said, "I was skating around for a full game, trying to pull my pants up."

In 1980, the NHL tried out a new design for hockey pants. These ankle-length pants were cool and lightweight. And they protected the pros from the knee up to the middle of the rib cage. After just two years, though, this invention was scrapped. The fabric ripped too easily.

And, when players fell, they slid along the ice dangerously fast.

The game itself has also changed since it began about 100 years ago. In the early days, teams played outside on frozen ponds. But when the game was taken inside, players had to watch for new dangers. Now, after every period, Zambonis clear loose snow and then spray water on the surface. Cold, hard ice means smooth, slick ice. Players can pass the puck more easily and skate faster than ever.

Today, players are big and strong. Short shifts allow them to display bursts of speed and power. The fastest skaters have been timed at 50 kilometres an hour. That's the speed limit for cars on Canadian city streets! When hockey players travel that fast, it's difficult for them to avoid danger. Accidents and injuries can happen without warning. Players don't always have enough time to react.

Safety Rules!

NHL rules have evolved, too. In the past, a player "iced the puck" when he sent the puck from his half of the ice, over the goal line at the other end of the rink. If an opponent touched the puck first, icing was called. Players would race to reach the puck first. They often collided with each other, or slammed into the boards. Now, the NHL has a "no-touch icing" rule. If the defending player can reach the dot inside the faceoff circle first, the ref calls icing. So now, players don't need to race to the goal line to reach the puck first.

2 Danger Between the Pipes

Even before November 1, 1959, Jacques Plante knew what it was like to be injured. Really injured. He said, "Pucks had already carved up my face for 200 stitches. My nose had been broken four times. Both cheekbones and my jaw had been fractured. Also a hairline skull fracture." But this goalie wasn't the first one to face danger night after night.

Growing up, Jacques's idol was Montreal's Bill Durnan. Bill played just seven seasons as goalie in the NHL, but he won the Vezina Trophy for the best goalie six times! Then, one day, Bill shocked everyone. He walked into his manager's office and announced, "I'm quitting."

"You can't quit now!" his boss said. "We're in the playoffs. We need you to help us win. You know where we stand. We're trailing in the series — three games to one."

But Bill had made up his mind. "I had broken my hand," he told a reporter. "And after it mended, it felt as if my arm was falling off whenever I'd catch the puck." The goalie had always been easygoing and calm under pressure. But things had changed. He said, "I was afraid I was blowing things." His nerves were shot, and it was time to go.

Those early days were a challenging time for rookies. Many capable players were eager to play. Teams didn't have backup goalies dressed and sitting on the bench, ready to play, as they do today. With six teams, and only one netminder for each, the entire league needed just six goalies altogether.

Refs stopped the clock so that wounded goalkeepers could be stitched up. But the rules allowed only 20 minutes for players to get the care they needed. When goalies were unable to return to the game, coaches had to choose one of the two goalies that the home team provided. These were called "house goalies." This was why injured goalies often refused to leave — even when they were seriously hurt. And they felt pressure to get back on the ice as soon as they could. They knew that their career could come to a quick end. They didn't want to be replaced. Those who didn't return were called cowards.

By the early 1950s, Bernie "Boom Boom" Geoffrion's slapshot had become famous. Before this, players relied on the wrist shot, the flip shot, or the backhand. The slapshot was the most dangerous because it wasn't very accurate. But it was fast and powerful. When a player took a slapshot, the hard rubber puck could travel faster than 160 kilometres an hour. Its speed gave the goalie little time to react. Because it was so popular, goalies were getting hurt more often than ever before. Many stopped goaltending to play other positions, or just quit hockey altogether. People called it "rubber shock."

Coaches and managers didn't want their goalies wearing masks. The New York Rangers' coach, Phil Watson said, "Who wants a good-looking goalie?" Others agreed. Montreal's general manager Frank Selke didn't like it either. He said, "A man has to be able to look at the puck face to face."

Goalies refused to wear masks. They

didn't want their teammates or fans to think that they were afraid. Glenn Hall was one of these goalies. Glenn played 502 straight games without missing one. That's more than seven whole seasons — with no mask! For goaltenders, he said, "Our first priority was staying alive. Our second was stopping the puck."

In net, he looked relaxed. But before almost every game, Glenn threw up into a bucket in the locker room. A teammate teased, "Your bucket should go to the Hall of Fame."

His defender Al MacNeil said to a reporter, "It was hard on all of them, playing without a mask when a deflection could literally kill you."

Still, Glenn refused to admit his fear. He said there was just one way to play the game: "That's at the very best of your ability, and I played better when I got sick."

Another time, he told the story of how a slapshot left a gash across both of his lips and knocked out a tooth. Thirty stitches later, the dentist said, "You're lucky!" Trying to talk through swollen lips, Glenn answered, "Ah don' fee' wucky!"

Years later, he sat down to speak with a sports reporter. Glenn explained that he learned to play with pain. "It was part of the game. It was part of the position . . . I still hate stitching with a passion . . . In the old days, they never used to freeze you."

After Jacques put on the mask, his boss, Frank Selke watched closely. He liked Jacques's winning record. Just one month later, he shocked reporters when he said, "Every goalie should wear a protective mask."

In 1962, superstar netminder Terry Sawchuk put on a game mask for the first time. Terry told reporters, "It has helped my game tremendously. I wouldn't be surprised if it added a few more years to my career."

That's when, one-by-one, other goaltenders decided to follow Jacques's lead. And finally, their coaches and general managers began to agree that this was a good idea.

One of the last goalies to put on a mask was New York Rangers' Lorne "Gump" Worsley. "Why don't you wear one?" reporters asked.

"It's not necessary. Why, all of a sudden, after hockey has been played for seventy years, do they decide we should wear masks?"

"The game has changed," someone dared to say.

"Aww, don't tell me that . . . Do boxers wear masks?" Gump growled.

Finally, he listened to his coach. "You better put on the mask and save your eyes."

But Gump didn't like it. He told reporters, "It was awful warm. And you still ducked."

Forwards and defenders refused to wear hockey helmets and visors for the same reasons. Comfort and pride were more important to them than safety. It was common to see players with scarred faces and missing teeth.

Scar Face

One evening, at team practice, goalie Gerry Cheevers was hit with a shot that "couldn't have broken an egg." Wanting to take a break from practice, Gerry went to the dressing room, pretending that he was badly hurt. There, he asked his trainer to draw a 30-stitch scar on his mask. "Look!" he told his teammates. "This is where I would have been hit — without my face protection." Over the years, Gerry added more "stitches." In time, he covered his mask in stitches.

3 The Man Behind the Mask

While still a little boy, Jacques Plante was diagnosed with asthma. When he skated, he often had trouble catching his breath. His friends said, "Stay in net. That's the best position for you."

He later said, "If it wasn't for my asthma, I would certainly have remained on defence, and possibly never have got beyond school hockey."

As a grown-up, he continued to battle asthma. But because he learned how to control it, he was still able to participate in his favourite sport. Jacques was careful to follow his doctor's advice by watching for symptoms, avoiding triggers, and taking his meds just as prescribed.

Jacques didn't mind admitting his fear of being hurt. He knew that didn't make him weak. "You can't be a goaltender and be afraid to get hit in the face. But you can't be a human being and not think about it," he said.

So he began wearing a mask during team practice. It took some experimenting. But, in time, he developed a mask that was just right. Jacques's first mask was plain white. It had two small holes for his eyes and one larger opening for his nose and mouth. It was lightweight, but strong. And because it was moulded to his face, he could see the puck coming at him from all angles. This is just what he wanted.

That night in 1959, the crowd had

been hushed — waiting, wondering, and worrying. Now, relieved to see Jacques return, everyone began singing, "For he's a jolly good fellow . . ." But when they saw his mask and the bloodstained sweater, they gasped. On the ice, the players heard a shout: "Hey, Plante, take that thing off. Halloween's over!"

November 1, 1959: Jacques Plante dares to be different, becoming the first goalie to wear a mask in a game.

The mask scared his opponents. Even his own teammates didn't like to look at him with it on. But the mask gave Jacques the confidence he needed. Now he could focus on saving goals. So, still in terrible pain, Jacques stayed in net right until the end. He allowed the Rangers to score just one goal, and helped his team win 3–1.

After the game, Coach Blake had to admit that his goaltender played well. He said that after Jacques put on the mask, it was his team's "finest game of the season."

Again, reporters surrounded the goalie. They wanted to ask about the mask, and they were eager to be the first to write about it in their papers. When he heard about the crowd's reaction, Jacques said, "I may look like Frankenstein, but I'm not out there to stop pucks with my face." He added, "I didn't care how the mask looked. The way things were going, I was afraid I would look just like the mask."

Soon, he and his teammates brought Montreal's unbeaten streak to eighteen straight games! How could Coach Blake say no after seeing what Jacques could do with the amazing mask?

Once, someone asked, "Doesn't the mask prove you're scared?"

Jacques answered, "If you jumped out of a plane without a parachute, would that make you brave?"

Another time, he told reporters, "My business is getting shot at . . . When I stop pucks, business is good. When I don't, business is bad. The mask doesn't help me to stop pucks, but when I don't have to worry about getting my face reshattered, I can concentrate on stopping them."

One reporter wrote, "He knows that he startles elderly ladies when he leers at them from the screens of their TV sets." But he needed the mask to survive.

Jacques had "simply decided he was too young to die."

It was the spring of 1970, 11 years after Jacques wore his game mask for the first time. The Stanley Cup finals were beginning, and Jacques's team was facing the Boston Bruins. Early in the second period, a slapshot hit Jacques in the face. His mask was destroyed.

At home, his two sons were watching the game. His wife, Jacqueline, had always refused to watch Jacques play. But near the end of this game, she came into the room and looked at the TV. She noticed that Jacques wasn't in the net. So she asked, "Where's your dad?"

Trying to act casual, the boys said, "Oh, he got hit with the puck. They carried him off the ice on a stretcher." Now, Jacqueline was worried.

Knowing how she would react, Jacques called his wife as soon as he could. Doctors said that he had a severe concussion. But Jacques was sure that he would be feeling better soon. He was more concerned about what people would say about the mask. He wondered, *Will they say it's a bad product? Maybe this is the proof they need.*

A nurse told him, "Too bad we'll lose you for the series, Mr. Plante. Your mask didn't save you this time, did it?"

He said, "My dear young lady, if it wasn't for my mask, you would now be gazing on me in a funeral home, not a hospital."

So, Jacques used his time in the hospital to improve his mask. He had been trying to invent one that made the puck bounce away, instead of becoming cracked or dented when the puck hit it. Now, he came up with an improved design.

It took time, but other goalies began to wear masks, too. In 1977, Gerry Desjardins was goaltender for the Buffalo Sabres. He was wearing a mask like Jacques's when he was hit in the face with the puck. Still, he suffered an eye injury. Sadly, this injury forced him to retire.

Then, two years later, Bernie Parent, goalie for the Philadelphia Flyers, was hurt. A stick got jammed in the eye opening of his mask. The sight in his right eye would never be the same. His doctors said, "Sorry, Bernie. But you have to leave hockey." He never returned to play.

After seeing Gerry and Bernie hurt, goalies began to put on a newly designed mask. This was the helmet and cage style — the same kind that netminders still wear today.

In 1999, *TIME* magazine named the ten most important athletes of the twentieth century. Jacques was the only hockey player on that list. And the only Canadian. "Gordie Howe was great, Bobby Orr greater, Wayne Gretzky the greatest."

Masterpieces

Today, goalies pay a lot of money to have artists paint their masks. Some have the team logo sprayed on. Others cover them with pictures of their favourite cartoon characters, buildings, or scenery.

But, the writer said that nothing changed hockey as much as "the piece of moulded fibreglass that Jacques Plante affixed to his head on November 1, 1959." Today, he is best remembered as the first goalie to wear a mask regularly in games. But his impact on hockey safety reached much further than that.

Jacques could be stubborn. For years, he made it clear that he disagreed with the "house goalie" rule. One day, on a train trip between games, he was speaking with the Canadiens' vice-president Ken Reardon. They began to argue about the

NHL's one-goalie system.

Jacques tried to convince his boss that one goalie shouldn't be expected to play every match of the season. He thought that each team should always have *two* goalies dressed and ready. Curious to hear what these two men had to say, reporters gathered around.

Reardon asked, "Why should the goalie be special? Don't all of the other players play seventy games unless they're injured?"

"You don't see baseball doing it. When a catcher is hurt, you don't borrow a catcher from the other team," Jacques said.

The news reporters nodded at each other. *He has a point,* they thought.

Then, in 1967, the league expanded to twelve teams. Now, everyone had to travel more than ever. So, teams began using the "two-goalie system." This is exactly what Jacques had fought for. It still is used today.

4 Reality Check

One of the most common injuries in hockey is a concussion. Surprisingly, goalies receive the fewest concussions. Centres get the most.

Another name for a concussion is traumatic brain injury (TBI). Any blow to the head can cause a TBI. Sometimes, a hit to the face or neck might also lead to a TBI. In hockey, this can happen when two players collide or when they fight. Or when a player falls to the ice. After the hit, the brain keeps moving rapidly inside the skull.

A concussion is called an "invisible injury." There are no cuts, bruises or broken bones. A headache is the most common warning sign. Hurt players might also feel dizzy or sick to their stomach. They might say that things look fuzzy. They may act confused or be unable to concentrate. Some people may feel sad or moody. They may be drowsy, or have a hard time falling asleep. In the worst cases, they may pass out. A person might have many of these symptoms, or just one.

In the past, coaches told players to "play through the pain" and "get back in the game" right away. But now, they know better. The brain is one of the most important organs. It controls everything the body does. This is why TBI is so dangerous.

Any person with TBI needs help right

away. This is true, no matter how many symptoms they have, or if they have no lasting symptoms at all. A delay might lead to more damage or a longer time to recover. "Treat each one seriously," doctors advise, "even when it's mild or minor."

Sadly, it took a tragedy before hockey players began thinking about ways to protect their brains. In January 1968, Bill Masterton was playing for the Minnesota North Stars. Then, one night, the rookie's career — and life — came to a sudden end. Like most players in the league at the time, he wasn't wearing a helmet. After he passed the puck, two players on the opposing team bodychecked him. He fell backward, hitting his bare head on the ice. Bill was carried off the ice on a stretcher. He never woke up again. The hockey world was shocked when the news came two days later. Bill had died in the hospital. He was the first person to die because of an injury in an NHL game. His injury: a concussion.

Now, players were scared. It was time for change. As one hockey writer said, Bill's death was "tragic, unnecessary, and foolish."

This horrible event took place almost nine years after Jacques had first put on his mask. But some coaches were still warning their goalies not to wear masks in games. Cesare Maniago, goalie for the Minnesota North Stars, told a reporter that after Bill died, the decision was easy. "I finally was able put a mask on." Many forwards and defenders began wearing helmets for the first time. Chicago's star forward, Stan Mikita, was one.

"Management was definitely against it," Stan said to the same reporter. He knew that if he put one on and his game "dipped the littlest bit," they'd blame the helmet. Still, he chose to wear one.

Bill's teammate and friend Ray Cullen added, "It's ridiculous that we thought that way back then, but we did. It took Bill dying for all of us to start thinking, 'What are we doing?'"

Surprisingly, it took eleven more years before the NHL told players that they *must* wear helmets. This rule finally passed in 1979. Even then, the rules committee grandfathered the rule in. This meant that they introduced it gradually. New players

The NHL Remembers

In the spring of 1968, the NHL paid a special tribute to Bill Masterton. They gave an award to the player who best showed sportsmanship and dedication to the game — like Bill did, all through his brief career. The Bill Masterton Memorial Trophy is still given out every year. Often, it goes to someone who faced an injury or illness.

had to begin wearing a helmet right away. But those with more experience could start wearing one when they chose. This way, in time, all would wear helmets.

Decades passed. Still, even with mandatory helmets, the number of TBIs did not go down. More competitors were getting hurt. Hurt athletes needed time to rest and heal. With popular players sitting out, ticket sales to games dropped. More importantly, some players never returned because their wounds were so severe. Worse yet, some had injuries that threatened to cut their lives short.

The NHL decision-makers were anxious. Public concern about player safety was growing. The league needed to act. So the top boss, Commissioner Gary Bettman, and all of the general managers got together. They had many questions. They wanted to know why head injuries still happened so often. They spoke with every team doctor across the league. They studied the numbers from seven regular seasons, from 1997 to 2004.

The group learned some interesting facts. Sometimes, players didn't report that they had TBI symptoms. Instead, they kept playing after a hit to the head. Later,

Bruins' star centre Patrice Bergeron in action.

they might tell someone about the injury. Sometimes, when they did take time off, players returned to play before they were fully healed.

But this kind of information wouldn't stop the growing problem. And Commissioner Bettman knew it. The league needed a plan. It would take a long time before they reached any real answers.

From the first time Boston Bruins' fans saw Patrice Bergeron play, they loved him. Patrice says that when he's with the team, he's doing what he loves. He told hockey writers, "Every time I step on the ice, I have that fire to go out and have fun, play the best I can and help my team to win." Reporters described his playing style as "always hard, always physical, and always clean." He played centre for the team.

Then, on October 27, 2007, the Boston newspapers shared some bad news. The Bruins lost 2–1 to the Philadelphia Flyers. But that wasn't the worst part. The story said that Bergeron had "a broken nose and a concussion after being hammered to the boards face-first" by Randy Jones.

Right after the hit, Patrice was knocked out. Doctors cut his jersey and took off his shoulder pads, and then put his neck in a brace. Gently, they lifted him onto a stretcher. Reporters said, "There was little sign of movement."

At the hospital, Patrice was awake, and moving his arms and legs. Teammates and coaches were relieved. Still, they wondered, *Has he played his last hockey game?*

Twelve days later, sportswriters met with the Bruins' centre and manager. They watched Patrice enter the room "carefully, while hunching over slightly."

A Boston reporter wrote that "his body said it all." The 22-year-old player had "the pace of an older man, using both hands as he climbed the steps" onto the platform.

To get better, Patrice needed rest. This meant resting his body *and* his brain. No reading, watching movies, or playing video games for him! He couldn't even watch his own team play hockey on TV.

When he was ready, he tried riding a stationary bike for five minutes. But even after these brief sessions, he got a headache. It was too much. He needed more rest.

A couple of months later, he met with reporters again. "When will you return?" they asked eagerly.

But Boston's centre refused to guess. "I don't want to rush things . . . The brain is the most important piece of your body and you don't want to mess with that."

So, Patrice did the right thing. Looking back, he said, "The doctors played the 'safe' card, and I'm glad they did. They put the human being ahead of the hockey player, and I am very thankful for that . . . I wanted to play — but I understood their position."

In June, hockey season ended, and teammates were planning their summer vacation. Patrice invited his friends to the arena to practise drills with him.

"Don't you realize that your hockey buddies are more interested in fishing, backyard barbecues, golf, and extra-extra-extra time by the pool?" reporters asked.

Patrice grinned. "Yeah, some of the guys are giving me pretty weird looks . . . But they know how I am, how long it's been for me, how much I miss it." He was determined to get back into game shape. So, he practised his skating, shooting, and stickhandling.

Finally, Patrice joined his team for the opening of the 2008–09 season. Unfortunately, he didn't stay long. Doctors say that after one concussion, another can happen easily. Just a couple of months into the new season, Patrice collided with an opponent. He crumpled to the ice. This was his second TBI.

At first, Patrice was frustrated because he had to go through the recovery process again. But he tried to stay positive. This time, Patrice wasn't knocked out, and he didn't experience all of the same symptoms. In fact, he was sent home from the hospital the next day. Still, Patrice knew that he needed time to fully recover. So, he carefully took the steps that he needed to take, so that he could to return to play — just like he did with his first concussion. And it worked! When doctors told him that he could return to the sport, he was ready.

5 Heads-Up!

The 2010–11 season was especially bad for head injuries. In October 2010, John Tavares was beginning his second year in the majors, playing for the New York Islanders. The accident happened in the first period of the very first game. John had been skating backwards. The TV announcer said Tavares was "in the middle of the ice, and he just got knocked off balance. He didn't really see it coming. And [Adam] Burish just sort of bumped into him." But John stood up and skated off the ice.

After the second period, the fans heard that Tavares had suffered a mild concussion and would not return that night. It was too early to tell when he could play again. But the centre followed the doctor's orders, and it wasn't long before he was back.

John never forgot what happened to him that night. He started thinking. *What is a concussion? Players need to know how to prevent them. If I — or one of my teammates or opponents — suffer a TBI, how can I recognize that? And what's the treatment?*

The Islanders' centre didn't realize it, but a team of medical professionals had been trying to find answers to these same questions. This group included Canadian sports medicine doctors, scientists, and concussion experts. These people knew that other NHLers respected John. He could have a major influence on player safety. So, they reached out to him. When they told him about their work, John was interested. They asked him, "Would you be willing to help us?"

John didn't hesitate. He knew that the NHL and the National Hockey League Players' Association (NHLPA) would think this was a great idea, too. Right away, he said, "Yes!" Patrice Bergeron also agreed to help.

John and Patrice had learned a lot

NHLPA

This group of past and present players takes care of the pros. They discuss salaries, benefits, and safety. First, the NHLPA holds votes to find out what the players want. Then, they tell the general managers and team owners. Together, they try to reach a deal. They want both sides to be happy. The NHLPA also encourages competitors to "give back" to their community.

from their experiences. They knew that prevention is the best cure for concussions. And education is the best way to keep them from happening. So, in March 2011, these two athletes appeared with other hockey stars in a video, called *ThinkFirst Smart Hockey*. Here, they talked to hockey coaches, trainers, and athletes. They discussed how to play safe and prevent TBIs.

For example, John knows how important it is to focus on the game. He wants to be aware of what's happening around him. By stickhandling with his head up, he always knows where the other players are. This can help him avoid a collision.

Todd McLellan, coach for the San Jose Sharks, agrees. He told a reporter, "We have to remind players not to expose themselves. The player receiving the check puts himself in that awful situation

. . . Anybody who has played hockey has been taught that you don't cut across the middle with your head down. You don't lunge and expose your head on a loose puck . . . I don't know if we're reminded enough about that these days."

Patrice's first brain injury happened when he was checked into the boards. Now, he uses his hands and arms as "shock absorbers." And because it's safer for his shoulders to take the impact, he tries to come at the boards on an angle, instead of head-on.

In the video, athletes also share advice on playing the game so it is safer for other players, too. To avoid giving an opponent a TBI, the pros think about their checking technique. John tells viewers, "You don't ever want to put your stick across somebody's back and push them from behind. This can cause injury to their head or neck. Same thing with your hands. Any time you see somebody's number with the back of their head to you, you want to avoid body contact."

Communicating with teammates is important, too. John advises all hockey players to assist their teammates this way to help them be safe. Other players might not realize when something is about to happen, but you might see it. "Give them a heads-up!" John says.

Wearing the best protective equipment is another way to prevent brain injuries. After his first concussion, Patrice talked with his team trainer about what he could do to protect his head even better. Then, together, they met with the company that made his helmets. He explained to reporters, "The people at Reebok are willing to help me a lot. They've been great. We've talked about the extra padding in there, and also to make sure that when it's on, it doesn't move." He needed a helmet that would be snug, but not tight.

Randy Jones received a two-game suspension for hitting Patrice from behind. Reporters asked Patrice, "What do you think about that?" Willing to forgive Randy, he said, "I don't have any anger towards him. But I just want to make sure it doesn't happen to anyone else . . . It's also for the kids. They're watching the game and they're watching us . . ."

Patrice has a reputation for "playing the right way." He continued, "It starts from the players. We all need to think about the consequences before we step on the ice . . . if you hit this guy from behind. Something bad can happen, so just don't do it. It comes down to you as a person and a player to take responsibility."

In the video, John and Patrice remind athletes that showing respect is the most important thing that any hockey player can do. John says, "You want to have that fine balance of being respectful and having that respect back." He knows that competitors want to do well. "But always, first and foremost . . . you want to make sure you're safe and healthy."

Lace 'Em Up!

Even during the off-season, John is thinking safety. His TBI happened when he was skating backwards. He admits that his skating ability was never his strong point. Reporters said that he had a great stride, but he wasn't fast or graceful. So, over the summer, he worked with a figure skating coach to improve his pivots and turns. Now, John is a strong skater. Regular practice keeps him safer in the game.

6 The Real Enforcer

While John and Patrice prepared their video, league leaders were busy, too. In 2011, they wrote a new set of rules. These rules explained how teams should deal with concussions. Now, any player bumped in the head must leave the game right away, and go to a quiet place nearby. There, a doctor — not a team trainer — must treat him. The league hoped that hurt athletes would be more willing to rest because they were farther from the "furious action and emotion" of the game.

Commissioner Bettman reported that the NHL was the first sports league with rules like this. The NHL also formed the Department of Player Safety. This new group had three jobs. Their number-one goal was to protect the players. Their second task was to deal with equipment issues. And their third concern was player discipline.

Then, the NHL announced that rule enforcer Colin Campbell was stepping down. They needed a new enforcer. Who could do the job? Who would deal with players who broke the rules? The league didn't have to look far.

Sportswriters had always enjoyed interviewing Brendan "Shanny" Shanahan. During his 21-year playing career, they often crowded around his locker to talk about his games. One reporter said, "Shanahan's influence was felt around the NHL." The media liked his honest answers. They could rely on him to say what was on his mind.

Like the hockey writers, the NHL had been watching Brendan closely. He was available because he had retired from playing just a couple of years before. He was a great leader — on and off the ice. They thought he was perfect for the job! The NHLPA agreed: Brendan would be fair. He understood what it was like to play pro hockey. At the same time, he would listen to what coaches, general managers, and other leaders had to say.

The NHL's new "top cop" was eager to get down to business. He thanked Colin Campbell "for the chance to have a positive impact on the game." Reporters smiled. But Campbell knew how tough the job was. He joked, "You won't be thanking me next year."

It wasn't long before Brendan found

out how true Campbell's words were. "My goal is to make the game as safe as possible," "Sheriff Shanny" explained. "I want to see head injuries dramatically come down. We can never get rid of all of them . . ." He told an interviewer, "I don't think it's a bad job." But he knew it would be tough, and he'd need "a thick skin." He said, "I have to stick with what I hope is best for the game and the future of these players."

Shanny watched replays of every game. He focussed on cross-checking, high-sticking, and hits to the head. He looked at everything from different angles. He decided which moves were all right and which ones were not. During an interview, he said that he and his new committee ask themselves, "Does the player have a history? Is this becoming repeat behaviour?" He said, "People have no idea how much we review . . . You have to know the difference between a two-minute slash, a five-minute slash, and a three-game suspension slash."

Shanny tried to be fair. He knew that the pros wanted to compete. He understood their passion. Sometimes, they needed just a warning. He thought back to his own game days. He always appreciated when Colin Campbell called him and said, "You know what? You're getting really close." That always helped Brendan.

He knew what it was like to make poor decisions "in split seconds." It's "a fine line," he said. He was looking for "good, clean, hard checks."

Sometimes, he sent emails to his group. His messages were to the point. "Thoughts?" he would ask. Then, the committee decided on the amount of "time for the crime." Finally, he reported to Commissioner Bettman and the NHL general managers.

Shanny also recorded videos. He showed replays of the hits. Then, he explained why the player deserved more punishment than the refs had given. *Maybe this way, I won't get so many angry phone calls late at night,* he hoped.

The sheriff liked the challenge. But it wasn't fun. He said, "You're not calling up a general manager to say, 'Hey, man! You guys were awesome . . .'" Sometimes, he sent players back to the minors. He hated to do that.

Soon, players realized that Brendan Shanahan meant business. He didn't hesitate to hand out penalties or suspensions for dangerous play. That's how he got his new nickname: Shana-ban.

Montreal Canadiens' defender Josh Gorges liked what Shanny was doing. "He's sending a clear message . . . Illegal blows aren't going to be tolerated. If guys haven't realized that by now, it's their own fault. It's a good move. Hopefully, it will save some guys from serious injuries."

Pittsburgh's captain Sidney Crosby had lost a lot of game time because of concussion symptoms. He agreed. "Whether it's accidental or not accidental, you've got to be responsible out there," he told a sportswriter.

It took time, but things began to improve. To prove this point, Shanny told a writer the story of how Pittsburgh Penguins' forward Matt Cooke asked to meet with him before the start of the season. Matt liked being a physical player. At the same time, though, he wanted to clean up his act. "He has seriously tried to change," Shanny said, but others "just don't seem to get it."

By 2012, the number of head shots was down. "Players are really getting it," Shanny reported. He liked the strides they'd made since the beginning of the season. "Change is always difficult . . . But we've got the best players in the world, the most talented. They can adapt, and for the most part, they are."

In the spring of 2014, the NHL made a big announcement. Brendan Shanahan was moving to Toronto, where he would become the president of the Maple Leafs. He was leaving his position with the Department of Player Safety. But the work that he had started would continue under a new leader.

By the end of the 2013–14 season, Commissioner Bettman reported that the number of concussions was lower that year. And players had missed fewer games. Bettman said that the league's rules were working. The NHL and the NHLPA are serious. More work needs to be done, but they are moving in the right direction.

The Perfect Set of Wheels

At 18, and brand new to the NHL, Brendan Shanahan needed a car to get to the arena. "I always liked Mustangs — a fun muscle car." So, that's exactly what he bought. Things changed, though, when he became Sheriff Shanny. Gone was the quick, powerful Mustang. In its place was a big sports utility vehicle (SUV) that he loaded with his three kids, their friends, hockey equipment, and his trusty dog. He said, "My cargo is more important than the look or the speed." Safety ruled. A fitting choice for the NHL's top cop!

7 A Blinding Shot

Sometimes, it takes a close call to change a person's mind about safety. This is exactly what happened with Vancouver Canucks' centre Manny Malhotra. The Canucks described their 2010–11 group as the best team in club history. Their third line was dominant, and Manny, a huge part of that line, was flawless in faceoffs, according to the team. He also knew how to kill penalties. Manny was their man.

Manny was living his dream. He told a

sportscaster, "The NHL is a fantasy life for us. We get to play a game that we grew up playing. It's our job now." This star centre had no idea that, in the blink of an eye, his dream was about to become a horrible nightmare.

On March 16, 2011, the Canucks were facing the Colorado Avalanche. The puck shot off an opponent's stick and flew straight up into Manny's face. Blood poured from his left eye. Manny fell. He was helped off the ice right away.

Later, Manny reported that, at first, it didn't seem like much. "I've had pucks in the face before. I've seen blood coming out of my face before. It didn't startle me all that bad . . . But to not be able to see right away threw me for a little bit of a loop. It started to get my nerves on end a little bit."

The injury turned out to be much more serious than he first thought. Doctors performed surgery right away. Three days later, Manny met with some of his teammates. A large white bandage covered his face. Then, the team announced that Malhotra would be out for the season.

His recovery didn't look promising. No one knew if he would ever play again. The NHL has a minimum vision requirement. Team manager Mike Gillis later reported that every time Manny stepped onto the ice, he'd be at risk. Manny might not see the puck or a stick — or another player — coming at him. Even "an innocent collision could be really damaging," Mr. Gillis worried. Manny could get hurt again. And the others on the ice could be in danger, too.

"Chances are slim," is all the doctors would say about a recovery. They were unwilling to predict whether the Vancouver centre would ever see well enough again. Team doctors agreed

The Secret of Willie O'Ree

Willie O'Ree, the first black person to play in the NHL, never forgot his older brother's advice. "If this is what you want to do, work towards it and don't let anyone tell you that you can't attain your goal . . . Be proud of who you are." So, Willie did what he'd set out to do. He played pro hockey for 20 years. Amazingly, though no one knew it at the time, he did it all with the sight of just one eye!

more surgeries were necessary. From the beginning, Manny knew that he would need time to recover. But he said, "I am very optimistic."

Surprisingly, less than three months after the injury, Manny was ready to return. Sportswriters wondered if it was too soon. But Manny had talked with the doctors. He said, "I wasn't flipping a coin in the change room deciding whether

I was going to play or not. They have assured me . . . everything continues to look good."

On June 4, Vancouver would face the Boston Bruins in Game 2 of the Stanley Cup finals. When Coach Alain Vigneault told him that he'd be in the lineup, Manny admitted, "It's probably the most nervous I've been in my entire career." But he just couldn't miss his first trip to the Stanley Cup championship round.

"Man-ny! Man-ny! Man-ny!" He came out of the dressing room, and skated onto the ice. Looking up into the stands, he saw a sea of white towels waving at him. The sound of the 18,000 fans in the Rogers Arena was almost deafening. "It was a pretty special feeling . . . But at the same time, it made me a little bit nervous that they were watching me that closely."

After the national anthems, the chants began again. This time, they were even

The youngest of four children, Manny Malhotra says his French Canadian mother and his South Asian father taught him that "there's no starting something, then giving up."

louder. Manny closed his eyes. He needed to concentrate. "I guess I really didn't settle down until after my first shift," he later told an interviewer. "That was hands-down the most memorable moment of my hockey career." He explained, "My family . . . and all the boys in the dressing room, they even got chills."

The faceoff ace was back. He played seven minutes and twenty-six seconds. His on-ice time was almost as long as the standing ovation the crowd had given him.

After the game, his coach told reporters, "He was good on the ice. He created a scoring chance."

Manny's return boosted his teammates' feelings. Alexandre Burrows said, "Two and a half months ago, we thought we wouldn't see him back. We were worried about his eye and his health. He's worked hard."

The Canucks' centre knew he had a long way to go. The first game back is "always a tough one," he said. But he knew that with time, he would improve.

"I'll start to try to make more plays, skate with the puck." He was happy to be back.

When Manny was hurt, teammates and even other NHL players took notice. Canucks' defender Kevin Bieksa reported, "Everybody feels for him . . . I've had friends on other teams ask me how he's doing that have never met him before."

One NHLer said, "You can break an arm and come back. You can shred a knee and come back. You lose an eye, you're done." On October 24, 2011, Chris Pronger of the Philadelphia Flyers discovered that this was true.

"Pronger has been hurt," the man calling the play-by-play said. "He's quickly going to the Flyers' dressing room. And he is screaming!" The reporter watched replays of the hit. Then he said, "The shaft of [Mikhail] Grabovski's stick went off the shaft of Pronger's, and came right up and hit him."

A sportswriter later said, "The blow was enough to send the Philadelphia Flyers' defender into a panic."

Chris suffered a concussion that night. The hit also left him unable to see out of the corners of his eye. If he wasn't looking straight at something, he couldn't see it at all.

He tried a brief comeback. But it was too soon. He still had concussion symptoms. Chris said, "It wasn't pretty." After five games, he needed a break.

At home, Chris's children were confused. For weeks, they begged, "Dad, when can we go to a game?" "Dad, when can you play?"

He answered, "I don't know. I want to get out there and play, too."

Then, the doctor told Chris, "Your vision will not get better." Chris had played his last NHL match.

Seeing Colour

Like Willie O'Ree, Manny knows what it's like to deal with racism. He grew up in Mississauga, which he says is "so multicultural . . . Jamaicans lived across the street. Asians were over there. It was a melting pot." Invited to speak at a high school ceremony, Manny told students, ". . . It never occurred to me that I was different. But when we went to some smaller cities for tournaments, I could hear a couple of racial slurs . . . My parents always taught me that if I reacted like them, I was no better than them."

8 The Great Debate

In less than a year, two major hockey stars — Manny Malhotra and Chris Pronger — suffered serious eye injuries. Now, NHL players, coaches, and decision-makers began to talk about eye safety. Change needed to come to the NHL. One reporter wrote that the idea of wearing a visor was a "hot-button issue going back many years." In fact, the debate began back in 1979 when the mandatory helmet rule came along.

Some players began to consider wearing eye protection for the first time. Willie Mitchell, Los Angeles Kings' defender, was one. A year before, Willie had suffered a concussion. Then, he had needed 53 stitches inside his mouth after a puck hit him in the face. When he saw what happened to Manny, he said, "It makes everyone think about wearing visors . . . What's the difference between me and Manny? Luck, right?"

When Manny returned, he thought differently, too. He says that now he wants to set a good example for his boys and for his team. So, he wears a visor. Hockey is "a very high-speed, high-impact game," he says. "And on a nightly basis, you see big hits on the highlight reel." Anything can happen in a split second. He knows that from experience.

Even hockey writers got in on the discussion. "These guys spend tens of thousands of dollars on personal trainers to get in the best physical condition possible," one reporter said. They want to "extend their careers and collect those million-dollar salaries for as long as they can. Yet they will not spend less than a hundred dollars to protect something vital to their careers."

For years, minor hockey leagues in Canada and the United States had said that players must wear face protection. But when pros joined the big league, they could decide whether they would wear cages or visors — or no face protection at all. A wire cage protects the entire face. A visor is like a windshield for the eyes. It covers the face just to the tip of the nose.

Toronto Maple Leafs' forward Nazem Kadri told an interviewer that in minor hockey, they "wore the cages all the time. I was excited to upgrade to a visor. I don't ever see myself today without a visor. It's nothing to do with toughness or strength. It's about eye safety."

Jarome Iginla agrees. When he joined the NHL, he chose not to wear a visor. But then he was hit in the face with a stick. "They said it was millimetres from being a lot more serious." That's when he decided it was time for him to put one on. He said to reporters, "It just wasn't worth it to me. Each guy has that decision. I don't find it's a big hindrance. I got used to it, and don't think of it."

Still, many chose not to wear this safety equipment at all. So, even though helmets protected their heads, hockey players still suffered injuries to the face. Eye injuries were common. Some were career-threatening, like Manny's. A few, like Chris's, were career-ending.

NHLers had all kinds of excuses for not wearing visors. Claude Julien, coach of the Boston Bruins, had heard most of them. Some players thought that when the opposing team saw them wearing a shield, they might be careless. They believed that more injuries might happen because of high-sticking. Julien admitted, "I know there's been some accidents." But he said that this was rare.

Others thought that eye shields would make them look weak. Julien said, "There's no stigma. I'm proud and I encourage guys to wear visors . . ." He knew young players coming up from minor hockey wore eye protection. "Why take it off?" he wondered.

For others, it was simply what they preferred. They liked the freedom they felt without a visor. One player said, "Somehow, not having to wipe the sweat off the visor, and 'feeling the air in your face' became more important."

It was only a matter of time before another player was seriously hurt.

Unfortunately, that's what it took to get everyone's attention.

On the night of March 5, 2013, the New York Rangers were facing the Philadelphia Flyers. When an opponent took a slapshot, the puck changed direction. Marc Staal had no chance. The puck hit him just above his right eye. The hurt Rangers' defender dropped to the ice. A trainer rushed out. With help, Marc skated to the bench, holding a bloody towel to his eye.

In the dressing room, Marc couldn't even see the doctor examining him. "I can see one dot of light. I can see one light bulb. But I can't see your hand, Doc. There's nothing there."

When Marc's older brother, Eric heard the reports and saw the replays, he said, "It's an awful feeling. And it made me sick to my stomach seeing him in that pain with his legs kicking." He reported that after he spoke with Marc, "He was in OK

spirits, but we don't know a lot right now
. . . We're saying prayers and hoping he
dodged a bullet."

Marc Staal warms up before a game. He and his three brothers, Eric, Jordan, and Jared, made it to the NHL.

Marc had many questions. His voice trembling, he asked, "Will I see again?" Then he wondered, "Will I ever play again?"

When doctors answered yes to both questions, Marc smiled. "I was lucky it wasn't worse."

His doctors just nodded.

In his first interview after the accident, he told reporters that he knew exactly how he could have avoided his injury. "It was the first thing that went through my mind when I hit the ice. I should have been wearing a visor. But hindsight is twenty-twenty."

It would take time to heal. Marc said, "My wife didn't sleep for the first four nights because she was just wiping blood off my eye."

The day after his first skating session, Marc said, "I could hardly get out of bed." He needed to get back into shape. He felt dizzy. Sometimes, his eye cramped up and he got headaches. "It was tough getting through a practice," he said.

So, he rested. He hated missing games, but he had no choice. The playoffs had started, and he wanted to be out there, helping his team. When he tried to return to play in the quarter finals, the symptoms returned.

"I don't think I'm quite ready," Marc told his coach the next day. "I've tried different medicine and eye drops." He told reporters that he didn't expect the eye to recover fully. But he planned to return as soon as doctors said he could.

Marc missed most of the 2012–13 season. Finally, after the summer, he said he felt "normal" for the first time since the hit. "I need to test myself in practices and scrimmages and games. I can't wait," he said.

His brother Jordan said that he'd

watched him skate, and "he's the same old Marc." The visor was the only thing that looked different. "He seems confident and ready to go."

Like Manny, Marc knows that players can't anticipate everything a puck will do. It travels at a high speed, bounces, and deflects. Anything can happen.

"Do you think that players should be forced to wear a visor?" reporters asked. The Rangers' defender knew that this would not be popular. He said, "Obviously guys don't want to wear it. I would probably be the same way if I didn't get hit." But he didn't want anybody else to go through what he'd been through.

So, when the NHLPA asked players what they thought about a new visor rule, he voted to make them mandatory "for *every* player *right now*."

His brother Eric thought it was too important. They shouldn't even be discussing if visors should be optional. "Smarten up," he said. "The best players in the world all wear one. They do fine."

The NHL and the NHLPA agreed that in the 2013–14 season, the mandatory visor rule would be grandfathered in. It would be like the helmet rule, back in 1979. This time, players who had played less than 25 games must begin wearing eye protection immediately. But players with more experience could decide for themselves.

So, the rule didn't go as far as Marc hoped, but it was a step in the right direction. NHLPA's Mathieu Schneider said that this was the first time ever that the "clear majority" voted in favour of a rule like this. Most NHLers were already wearing eye guards. After seeing what had happened to Manny, Chris, and Marc, others decided it was time for them to change their habit.

Mathieu told the media, "Every time there's an injury like that, any player playing without a visor starts to think about it. Or has his mom calling him, or his wife and kids . . . It's the reason why the numbers are so high. More guys put a visor on after the Staal injury."

"One-Eyed Frank"

Frank McGee got his nickname when he was injured in a hockey game and lost the sight in his left eye. The league's "first superstar," Frank played in the NHL during the early 1900s. That was before the vision rule came along. A fellow NHLer recalled, "He was even better than they say he was. He had everything — speed, stickhandling, scoring ability, and was a punishing checker."

9 In a Heartbeat

Each year, about 40,000 Canadians have a sudden cardiac arrest (SCA). And only about 2,000 survive. There's no doubt: SCA is a medical emergency. It can strike anyone at any time, without warning. It can even affect young people who are in good shape.

How can you help a person who suffers an SCA? The first step is always to call 9-1-1. Then, a trained person should give cardiopulmonary resuscitation (CPR) to help blood get to the heart. This can help the person stay alive until medical aid arrives. It can also protect the brain and other organs from harm. If an automated external defibrillator (AED) is close by, the trained helper should use that, too. The AED "shocks" the heart into beating regularly again.

Atrial fibrillation (AF) is a common heart disorder. And it's the most common cause for SCAs. Other names for AF are "irregular heartbeat" and "rapid heartbeat." Although it strikes older people most often, it can affect younger people, too, even talented hockey players like "Super Mario" — Mario Lemieux.

Mario Lemieux spent all of his pro hockey life playing with the Pittsburgh Penguins. He was considered one of the greatest players ever to play the game. All through his career, Mario battled back and hip injuries. Sometimes, his back pain was

Mario Lemieux joined the Penguins at 19, and scored his first goal on his first shift in his first game! Now, he owns the team.

so bad that he couldn't tie his own skates. Often, he had to ask the trainer to do that for him. Somehow, he continued to play, despite the pain. "It was better than sitting in the stands," he said. Then, after one surgery, he got a rare bone infection. His doctor told him that he might never walk again. Still, he did return and helped his team win the Stanley Cup two years in a row.

Then in January 1993, doctors told him that he had Hodgkin's disease, a form of cancer. This was difficult news to accept. But Mario was determined to beat it. He rested and got his treatments. Amazingly, he took just two months away from the ice.

Super Mario Comes up with a Plan

Mario Lemieux knows firsthand what it's like to fight cancer. He says that his battle showed him two things: "how fragile life can be . . . and how fortunate I am to be involved with the greatest game in the world . . ." So, he decided to take action. He set up the Mario Lemieux Foundation. Now, he has just one goal on his mind: to find a cure.

In 1997, Super Mario left hockey. Three years later, he was back. He couldn't stay away from the game he loved. "The league needs guys like that," another NHLer said. "Their impact on the game is just tremendous." One broadcaster said, "After you look back and reflect on his career and know the situation of all the things that he's gone through . . . you gotta put an A+ up there . . . He continues to have the courage of a lion, every day of his life."

Then, in 2005, another setback came along. When doctors told Mario that he had AF, he decided that it was time to quit. He retired for the second time in 2006. This time, he wouldn't return.

From the start of his NHL playing career, the Pittsburgh captain had avoided the media. "That's the way I want it. The less people know about me, the better," Mario always said. But in January 2010, he chose to speak in an interview. He thought that hockey fans deserved to know more. So, he spoke openly about his condition. He decided that this was an opportunity for him to help others who have the same symptoms he did while he was playing hockey. So, he told people about AF. "It feels like your heart wants to jump out of your chest. It's pretty scary . . . The palpitations are strong. You can see your heart moving, your chest beating."

When a person has AF, they may suddenly feel out of breath, tired, or dizzy. Doctors say that a person might have symptoms one day, then be okay for months. At first, Mario ignored the warning signs — even his racing heart. He thought that he was just dehydrated. So, he drank fluids. After about an hour, he felt better. He didn't report anything to his doctor. This made it hard for his doctor to detect.

Now, Mario says the best advice is: "Go see your doctor right away . . . and not wait a few months like I did." Usually, doctors can treat the condition with medicine. Untreated, AF can lead to a stroke or even death.

It's a good thing that Mario was willing explain his reason for retiring. Without realizing it, he had a major influence on the health and safety of people of all ages, all across North America. His willingness to share his message led to many lives being saved — both on and off the ice. AF led to the end of Super Mario's playing career. But something even bigger was just beginning.

From the time Chase McEachern was a little boy, he was a hockey fan. When he was three years old, he learned how to skate. At the age of five, he scored 130 goals for his local team. Soon, the left wing was named the team's assistant captain. Not only did he enjoy playing the game, he also loved to watch his favourite player, Sidney Crosby, play on TV. He liked to read about hockey heroes, too.

But when he was 11, Chase was hurt in a football game at school. During his stay at the Toronto SickKids hospital, specialists did tests. By chance, they discovered that Chase had AF. Even when he was just sitting still, his heart raced. Sometimes, it would beat 150 times in a minute. "This is a serious condition. And he'll need surgery," the doctor told Mr. and Mrs. McEachern. The doctor explained that the operation is called a cardioversion. Surgeons would help bring Chase's heart rhythm back to normal by putting in an electric pulse.

"We know the first question he'll ask when we tell him the news. What will we say? Will he be able to keep playing hockey?" his parents asked.

"Yes, for now," the doctor answered. "But he'll have to wear a heart monitor for a while so we know how his heart is behaving."

The next day, the doctors performed the surgery. It went well. Then, in a few days, Chase returned home. When he was strong enough, he went back to school, and happily joined his team at the rink.

It wasn't long before Chase wasn't feeling well again. The heart monitor showed that during team practice, his heart beat almost 320 times a minute. Chase needed to be taken back to the hospital. It looked like Chase's hockey days might be over. Troubled, Mr. and Mrs. McEachern talked as they drove home. "We need to tell him," Chase's dad said. "Yes, but how will he react?" Mrs. McEachern wondered.

Chase's parents were surprised at his reaction. Instead of becoming discouraged when he heard the news, he decided to learn all he could about the disease. "Maybe I'm just a kid. But there's got to be something I can do so other boys and girls don't have to worry about this."

Then, on TV, he saw what happened to Jiri Fischer, a powerful defender for the Detroit Red Wings. During the game on November 21, 2005, Jiri collapsed on the bench. He was having a cardiac arrest. Unconscious for six minutes, Jiri was revived with the help of CPR and an AED. An AED saved Jiri's life!

When Chase found out that Mario Lemieux had the same illness that he had, he became even more interested. "What if this had happened to me?" he wondered. "This isn't something that just happens to older people. We need more AEDs available in more public places. Places like hockey arenas and schools."

Now, Chase was excited. *Here's my*

Stayin' Alive

When Jiri Fischer collapsed of cardiac arrest, Brendan Shanahan and Mathieu Schneider played with him on the same team. Brendan said that the doctor was giving Jiri CPR before he even knew which one of his teammates was down.

Mathieu recalled, "That was one of the scariest moments of my career . . . It was a great effort to save him."

answer, he thought. *This is something I can do!* And he didn't waste any time. After telling his parents about what he had seen, he got to work. He came up with a plan. Chase was determined to save more lives.

Chase had covered the desk in his bedroom with a drawing of a hockey rink. Sitting at his desk, he wrote a letter to Don Cherry. Chase knew that February was Healthy Heart Month. He thought this would be the perfect time for Mr.

Cherry to raise awareness. So, in his letter, he asked, "Please read this on Coach's Corner in February." Then, the hockey fan set the page aside to edit later.

February 9 started out just like any normal school day. Chase went with his class to the gym, and began running laps to warm up. When Chase's teachers saw him fall suddenly, they knew exactly what to do. They called 9-1-1. The ambulance arrived, and paramedics rushed him to the hospital. There, the young hockey player slipped into a coma.

While Chase was in the hospital, Mr. McEachern found the letter on his son's desk at home. Right away, his father delivered it to Don Cherry. Sadly, Chase never heard Don read his letter.

On February 15, 2006, the day after Valentine's Day, Chase died. He was a month away from his twelfth birthday. Chase had lost his battle with heart disease.

Knowing how important AEDs could be to people of all ages, Chase had begun to change the game of hockey by fighting to get them in all schools and arenas. Now, it was up to Don Cherry.

10 Playing with Heart

"Dear Mr. Cherry, My name is Chase McEachern. I play hockey for my local Minor PeeWee AAA team. I've heard about Mario Lemieux, and I hope you can help me. I've started a campaign . . ."

The words caught Don Cherry's attention. It was late, time for him to get to bed. Instead, he kept reading the letter from the young fan. Finally, he came to the end. Wiping tears from his eyes, Don put the paper down on his desk.

As soon as he'd finished reading Chase's words, the outspoken "tough guy" knew he had to do something to help. Talking about it on Coach's Corner was the best way he knew. *Just wait 'til Saturday night,* he thought. *I'll tell the world.* And he did. Exactly as Chase had hoped, Don Cherry, or "Grapes" as he is known, shared his story with hockey fans everywhere.

In 2011, five years later, Chase would have turned 17. On February 15, Don Cherry and Mr. McEachern made a special trip to the Hockey Hall of Fame in Toronto. They were going to celebrate Chase's work. On that day, an AED was displayed there in his honour. By that time, 2,700 AEDs had been set up across Ontario. Still, Mr. McEachern said, "More needs to be done." Grapes agreed.

Later that year, NHLPA and the Heart and Stroke Foundation joined forces. They hadn't forgotten Chase's dream.

Chase McEachern inspired Don Cherry to make a difference.

They decided that they would set out to make Canada "the most heart-safe country in the world." That playoff season, they raised enough money to put twenty-nine new AEDs in arenas across Canada.

Chase's parents and brother, Cole, set up the Chase McEachern Tribute Fund. Through this, Chase's work lives on. Together, they encourage politicians and business people to do what they can to help.

In 2013, Prime Minister Stephen Harper announced that the Canadian government would work with the Heart and Stroke Foundation. Their goal was to put AEDs in every hockey arena across Canada, and to train staff how to use them properly. A hockey fan, Harper said that the government was "committed to protecting the health and safety of Canadians while encouraging active and healthy lifestyles."

Reporters asked him, "Don't athletes

in other sports need this equipment, too?"

The prime minister said, "Yes, they do." But he explained that they chose hockey because it's high risk. Cardiac events are "unfortunately common in hockey rinks because it is such a high stress sport." He planned to start here. Then, in the future, he'd ask where else in a community you could put a defibrillator. Harper realized that AEDs need to be available when people have an SCA.

On March 10, 2014, the NHL saw once more how important Chase's goal was. The Dallas Stars were hosting the Columbus Blue Jackets. Just six minutes after the first faceoff, Rich Peverley had finished his shift. Back on the Stars' bench, he struggled to catch his breath. Suddenly, he slumped over. A few people in the arena noticed that something terrible had happened. The crowd was silent. Rich needed help right away. Teammates started banging their sticks against the boards. They had to stop the game! When that didn't work, they all jumped over the boards and onto the ice. This was life or death. It worked.

The team doctor used the nearby AED. As soon as he treated Rich, he was alert and awake again.

Coach Lindy Ruff told sportswriters that the medical team "deserved a standing ovation." He was pleased to hear Rich speak. Coach Ruff said, "The first thing he asked me was, 'How much time left in the first period?'" It looked like Rich would be all right.

Like Chase, Rich had surgery to correct his AF. Just a couple of weeks later, doctors told him, "The operation was successful. You can begin working out."

In July, Rich shared an update. "I'm lucky to be here!" he told friends and fans. Although he wants to play hockey, he said,

"There is a chapter after hockey, if that's the road we go down. But we'll wait and see what happens. I'm just excited to see where it's going to take me next."

Grapes Speaks Out

Don Cherry started out as a "physical" player. After an NHL coaching career, he sold his popular Rock'em, Sock'em Hockey videos. Soon, Grapes got a new job with *Hockey Night in Canada*, as co-host on Coach's Corner. Here, he became a familiar face to fans everywhere. He talked about his favourite players. He reviewed plays that he liked. Sometimes, he talked about injuries. And he fought to bring "no-touch icing" to the NHL. Grapes always said exactly what he thought.

11 A Stroke of Bad Luck

Pro hockey players know that fans love to watch them play. They remember what it was like to see their own hockey heroes on TV. They also realize that people are interested in what they do off the ice, too. So, the NHLPA encourages players to get involved in community events. They can use their fame to make a difference in the lives of others.

Some hockey stars have started their own charities when they or a family member became sick or injured. These players raise money for life-saving research. The NHL helps by providing links to their websites. The players hope that one day, these serious health issues will be gone.

Every spring, when playoff season begins, hockey players stop shaving and begin to grow their "playoff beard." They don't shave it off until one of two things happens. Either their team is

Star Power

In July 2014, P. K. Subban, Drew Doughty, and Corey Perry joined Brandon Prust in a round of golf. This was the second annual Prusty 4 Kids golf tournament. The money they raised went to the Kids Kicking Cancer program. Brandon says, "To see kids struggling with serious illnesses, but finding a way to smile and be strong, it really affects you. It makes you want to help out, to give back, to do something positive for them."

bumped out of the playoffs, or they win the Stanley Cup. NHL finalists — and even competitors in other leagues across Canada and the United States — take part in this tradition. Some do it because they think it will help their team win. Others just do it for fun. But they all consider their beards a symbol that shows their passion and spirit of the playoffs.

Seeing how popular this was, the NHLPA held their first Beard-A-Thon in 2011. This was the perfect chance to raise money for a good cause. Now, when players "give their razor a rest," they encourage others to join in on the fun. Fans and players compete to grow the best beard, and teams raise money by collecting pledges. Beard-A-Thons have raised money for charities like the Canadian Cancer Society and the Heart and Stroke Foundation.

Some might think that it's just older

people who suffer a heart attack or stroke. Or people who are unhealthy. But this isn't always the case. Just ask Kris Letang. He never thought an emergency like this would happen to him. On January 29, 2014, the Pittsburgh Penguins' defender was at the peak of his career. Kris was young and fit. Life was good.

But early that cold winter morning, the 26-year-old hockey player knew that

The strongest skater on his team, Kris Letang loves to compete.

something was wrong. He didn't know what it was then, but he had suffered a stroke. When his wife, Catherine, woke up, she found him lying on the bedroom floor, unable to move. Doctors discovered that Kris had been born with a small hole in his heart. Every baby has this condition before they are born, and for most, the hole closes on its own. For Kris, it didn't close. This might have been the reason for his stroke.

Kris said, "It was a shock to get the news, but I'm optimistic that I can overcome this." The Penguins' coaches, managers, and players couldn't believe the news either. "I don't know a whole lot about a stroke, or what causes it," defender Matt Niskanen said.

Their captain Sidney Crosby agreed, "It's surprising for somebody his age, and it's not something you typically hear, especially with a guy who takes so good care of himself . . ."

In some ways, Kris has a lot in common with his boss, Mario Lemieux, now a co-owner of the Penguins. Like Mario, he prefers to get attention by what he does at the rink instead of what he says in interviews. But since his stroke, he's changed his mind. Now, Kris, too, believes it's important to share his story. He says, "I hope that by making my condition public . . . I can help other people." He encourages anyone experiencing stroke symptoms to seek medical help. Whatever their age or health.

But unlike Mario, the Penguins' defender was able to return. Kris showed the hockey world that his stroke wouldn't force him to leave the sport. He said, "My first reaction was, 'When would I skate again and play again?'" Sure enough, by early April, he was ready.

On the evening of his return, reporters

Taking it a Step Further

Just a few months after his stroke, Kris decided he needed to take action. So, he joined the Heart and Stroke Foundation. Now, he works with them as co-chair of their annual walk in Pittsburgh. They have two goals. They want to tell more people about heart disease and strokes. And they try to raise money to learn more about these health issues. Kris challenges fans to walk along with their family, friends, and co-workers. He wants everyone to "choose to build a healthier life and a healthier community."

surrounded him. They were eager to hear what the Pittsburgh player had to say. Sitting in the locker room, with bright lights, mics, and cameras in his face, he smiled and waited. The questions kept coming. "How do you know you're ready?" "What does your family think?"

"Aren't you afraid it could happen again?" He knew that these journalists had a job to do. His return was big news, and they were in a race to get it to the public first.

One by one, he answered each question. He explained that he always wanted to come back. His family was scared. But doctors said he could play.

As for how Kris himself felt about his recovery, he said, "I feel one hundred per cent able to deal with it . . . I'm nervous. It's been a long time without playing. But about my situation, not at all."

The sportswriters asked him what the doctors had said. "Right from the start, they told me it could happen whenever — sitting around, walking around." He wasn't worried.

"I'm not gonna lie . . . I was kind of scared to make mistakes," Kris admitted later. "I was a little bit on my heels, trying to accomplish too much . . ." After his first few games, though, he felt like he'd returned to playing the way he did before the stroke. "My game is being aggressive and skating and being in the play all the time and supporting my forwards. Once I was able to do that, my game kind of changed."

Coach Dan Bylsma was surprised at Kris's quick return. It was "a blessing" to see him out there, he said.

Teammates, too, were happy. Centre Brandon Sutter said it was "a couple of tough months for him. It was scary for everyone . . . but he's been great since he's come back. We definitely need him . . ."

With Kris's help, the Pittsburgh Penguins reached the second round of the 2013–14 season playoffs. Later that spring, the team chose Kris as their "comeback player" of the year. So, he was nominated for the Bill Masterton Memorial Trophy.

Epilogue

The Pittsburgh Penguins' captain Sidney Crosby has been around hockey long enough to know that the game can take its toll on a player's body. For him, safety begins with his hockey gear. You want "any edge you can gain," he says. "In your footwear or your equipment. It can help you prevent injuries or pressure on your joints."

The Penguins' equipment manager says, "All his gear is customized." He puts

Sidney Crosby celebrates winning the ultimate prize in hockey with his goalie, Marc-Andre Fleury.

Loctite on Sid's skates so Sid isn't distracted by a clicking sound when he skates. And every two weeks, he gets brand-new blades. When Sid finds protective gear that he likes, he uses the same pieces of equipment. Sometimes, for years.

From the beginning, Mario Lemieux was impressed with Sid's "passion for the game and his will to be the best each and every shift." That's because for Sid, winning is everything. He says, "Losing stinks. It really does." When he and his team are not playing consistently, he gets frustrated. "It's no fun having personal success while we struggle as a team."

So, the Penguins' captain leads by example. Even during the off-season, Sid is passionate about keeping in his best shape. He works out to prevent injuries. He hopes that by being stronger and better prepared for a long season, he'll be healthier and able to play more games.

Even though Sid does everything he can to avoid getting hurt, accidents happen. And he has suffered some major injuries. His first came in January 2008. He slid into the boards and hurt his ankle. That night, the announcer said, "He gets up very gingerly . . . He's being helped off the ice . . . He seems to be in a boatload of pain."

A Diet Fit for a Pro

Eating right can improve strength and performance. Sid admitted to sportswriters that sometimes, he'll eat "the odd piece of cake, here or there, or ice cream . . ." But he knows that making "little sacrifices" is worth it. "It's not a big deal once you get in the routine," he says.

Montreal Canadiens' defender P. K. Subban uses his off-season to stay fit and healthy. Just like Sid. He eats his veggies and "steak in the morning, steak in the afternoon, fish, chicken."

"You can tell when you're hurt," Sid said later. "I just hoped it wasn't too serious." But Sid refused to predict when he might return. He told sportswriters, "I want to make sure that when I do come back it's healed enough where if I do tweak it a bit, it's not going to bring me back to square one. That's something that

I don't want to go through."

While recovering, he still went to the Penguins' dressing room before games. "I'm hurt, but that doesn't mean I'm gone." Sitting out wasn't easy. He told reporters, "It was eating me up not being out there. The mental aspect of being hurt is tougher than the physical."

Mario reminded him, "Be patient. You're going to have a long career." One or two weeks wouldn't change anything.

So, Sid followed his boss's advice, and two months later, he was back. That night, Sid wasn't the only one excited about his return. Reporters said that day was "like Christmas on March 4" for hockey fans.

But soon, at morning skate, Sid told his coach, "something doesn't feel right in my ankle." He said, "I wasn't about to take any chances. Neither were the doctors. And just like that, after three games, I was back on the shelf."

Since then, Sid missed most of the 2010–11 and 2011–12 seasons. This time, concussion symptoms kept him away. When the 2012 World Championships came, Sid was invited to play for Team Canada. But when Sid opted out, some fans were puzzled. Some were disappointed. When reporters asked him why, Sid was surprised. More than anything, he wanted to get back out onto the ice and play. But he knew it would take just one thing to come back: time.

Then a slapshot hit Sid in the mouth. Several teeth were knocked out and he suffered a broken jaw.

But in June 2014, Sidney again proved that big injuries don't always mean the end of a hockey career. Two years earlier, Sid was recovering from a concussion, and hoping that one day, he could return to the ice. He had done everything that the experts tell athletes to do. Now, he was celebrating the end of the NHL season with the other players. It was awards night. As one reporter wrote, "Healthy Crosby Cleans Up . . ." Yes, he was on stage — accepting not one, not two, but *three* top awards.

Sidney explained why he had such a great season. He said, "You need a lot of things to go right. You need to play with a lot of good players. You need to stay healthy. I'm happy to be able to do that this year."

Thanks to the game-changers that came before him, Sidney was able to focus on playing his game. But researchers are continuing look for ways to improve hockey safety. Companies pay big money to people to develop new products for them. Doctors constantly look for better ways to treat illness and injuries. Just think what the hockey stars of tomorrow will be able to do!

Glossary

Asthma: A lifelong condition. A person having an asthma attack might have difficulty breathing. Asthma is usually treated with medicine.

Atrial fibrillation (AF): A common heart disorder, also called "irregular heartbeat" or "rapid heartbeat."

Automated external defibrillator (AED): An electronic device that "shocks" the heart into beating regularly again.

Backup goalie: A player who travels with the team and is available to play if the starting goalie leaves the game because of an injury, or if the coach pulls the starting goalie out because of a poor performance.

Bill Masterton Memorial Trophy: An award named after Bill Masterton, the first person to die because of an injury in an NHL game. Every year, the NHL chooses one player who displayed "perseverance, sportsmanship, and dedication to hockey." Often, it goes to a player who battled injury or illness.

Centre: A forward who plays most of the game near the centre of the ice. The centre usually takes the faceoffs.

Cardiopulmonary resuscitation (CPR): When someone has a sudden cardiac arrest (SCA), a trained person uses this medical procedure to help get blood to the heart. This is done by pumping the patient's chest, and breathing into the mouth.

Concussion: Also called traumatic brain injury (TBI), a concussion is an injury to the brain. It is caused by a blow to the head, face, or neck.

Defender: Also called "defence," a defender's main task is to assist the goalie by clearing the puck out of the zone in front of the net.

Deflection: When a puck hits an object or a person, and it changes direction.

Faceoff: When a player scores a goal, gets a penalty, or is injured, the ref blows the whistle to stop play. In order to start playing again, the centres on the two teams face each other with their sticks on the ice. After the ref drops the puck, they both try to "win" the faceoff by being the first to touch the puck with their stick.

Forward: This player's main job is to score goals or assists. There are three places where a forward can play: left wing, centre, or right wing.

Goalie: Also called "goaltender" or "netminder," this player tries to keep the opposing team from scoring. To do this, she must stop the puck from crossing the goal line and going into her net.

Grandfathering: Introducing a rule gradually, starting with new players and giving more experienced players time to adjust.

Icing: Occurs when a defending player shoots the puck from his half of the ice, over the goal line at the other end of the rink.

National Hockey League Players' Association (NHLPA): This organization communicates with the general managers and team owners. Their reps look after the needs of the players. Current and past players form the group.

Playoffs: The Stanley Cup playoffs are played by the teams with the most wins to determine the winner of the cup.

Poke check: Occurs when a player uses his stick to "poke" the puck away from an opponent.

Regular Season: Currently each team in

the NHL plays 82 games in the regular season.

Slapshot: The most powerful shot that a hockey player can take. It's fast and dangerous. To shoot a slapshot, the player raises his stick high in the air, and then lowers it quickly to "slap" the puck as hard as he can.

Stroke: A medical emergency. Usually, when a person has a stroke, their blood doesn't flow normally to the brain.

Sudden cardiac arrest (SCA): A medical emergency. A person having an SCA will usually collapse. She will be unable to respond to touch or sound, and she'll stop breathing normally.

Traumatic brain injury (TBI): See "Concussion" above.

Vezina Trophy: An award for an outstanding NHL goalie, named after Georges Vezina, goalie for the Montreal Canadiens from 1910 to 1926.

Visor: Attached to the helmet, this piece of equipment allows the hockey player to see, while protecting his eyes. A cage does the same job, but the visor is the more popular choice of eye protection in the NHL.

Acknowledgements

While playing for the Toronto Maple Leafs, near the end of his career, Jacques Plante received approximately 200 fan letters every day. My husband, Jonathan, was one of the fans who asked him for goaltending advice. When I heard that Jacques had taken the time to respond to Jonathan personally, Jacques become my sports hero, too. That story sparked the idea for this book.

In some cases, I presented dialogue that was not quoted word-for-word, but sources indicated that this is what the people said at the time.

As I conducted my research, I relied on a few sources for their excellent quotes, as well as details about equipment, games, injuries, and comebacks. These were www.nhl.com, www.hhof.com, and the Legends of Hockey videos. Other great sources were CBC, Global News, TSN, Sportsnet, Yahoo Sports, the NHLPA, and the Ontario Hockey League. Thanks to Craig Campbell, who kindly shared additional resources from the Hockey Hall of Fame.

I discovered useful information about health and safety issues from Parachute Canada, Ontario Ministry of Health, Afib Treatment Today at www.afibtreatment.com, and the Office of the Prime Minister at www.pm.gc.ca. Hockey Canada and Pro Hockey Stuff supplied information about equipment.

I couldn't have written this book without *The Jacques Plante Story* (McGraw-Hill Ryerson, 1972), written by Andy O'Brien with Jacques Plante, and *Jacques Plante: The Man Who Changed the Face of Hockey* (McClelland and Stewart, 2009), by Todd Denault. In the sections about Jacques Plante, any quote where the source is not mentioned came from one of these books.

Other books that supplied many valuable quotes include *Hockey Hall of Fame Legends: The Official Book* (Viking Studio, 1995) by Michael McKinley; and the NHL's booklet, *The History of Hockey Equipment* (2007).

The following newspapers and magazines detailed the amazing stories of the athletes: *Boston Globe*, *Calgary Sun*, *Canadian Living*, *Dallas Morning News*, *Globe and Mail*, *Hamilton Spectator*, *Hockey News*, *Kitchener Record*, *Maclean's*, *Metro News*, *National Post*, *New York Post*, *Reader's Digest*, *Ottawa Sun*, *San Jose Mercury News*, *Sports Illustrated*, *TIME*, *Toronto Life*, *Toronto Star*, *Vancouver Sun*, and *Winnipeg Sun*.

I appreciate the assistance that Linda Staal and John and Dorothy McEachern gave as I prepared this book. I'd also like to thank Andrew Parish and Karen Arnold of the Mario Lemieux Foundation, as well as Stephanie Lawrence and Rhae Ann Bromley of the Heart and Stroke Foundation of Canada for their efforts and encouragement.

Finally, a big thanks to Christie Harkin, who helped me get started on this project, and to Kat Mototsune, my editor, and the whole team at Lorimer for all their help.

About the Author

SUE IRWIN teaches in Hamilton, Ontario. Her writing has been published in a variety of children's publications and has won several awards. A lifetime hockey fan, Sue lives in the Niagara region with her husband, and spends her winter evenings cheering for her favourite hockey players

Photo Credits

Index